# Acknowledgm[illegible]

I want to thank eve[illegible] understanding, kindn[illegible] [illegible]pport they provided me with through this horrific chapter of my life.

To all my family members, friends and their friends, my dogs, even strangers at times, and some of my doctors, you have all contributed to my success of getting clean, staying clean, and bringing back some normalcy to my life.

Most, but not all, have been mentioned in my book at some point. For those who are not mentioned, I know who you are, and you are greatly appreciated and loved. As much as I would like to name you all individually, it would be a never-ending list of personal angels.

During my addiction and withdrawal, everyone who was aware of my situation always made every effort to do what they could to make me comfortable, even if it was the smallest of things, like letting me sit in the front seat of the car or serving me food. Even some of the minor things were the most difficult for me.

During this time, the people who shared my life had a knack for knowing when I was either down and depressed or in pain. They learned how to pick up my spirits or when just to let me be. That was not actually as easy as you would think, considering how erratic my personality had become.

Special thanks to my loved ones who had to live with me and endured all my shit day-in and day-out for all those years. Although they really didn't have a choice, they accepted it and dealt with it in their own ways. I know they all still have bad memories that can't be erased, forgotten, or forgiven, but most have all moved on from those dark days. I owe my life to every single one of you, and I will be forever indebted to you.

God bless you all!

## Special Thanks

I want to give a special shout-out to three people that contributed greatly to getting my book published.

First, is my eldest son Brett. He provided his professional expertise in radio production along with his natural radio voice to narrate and produce the Audible version of this book. Having him do the narration was very special to me.

Second is his wife, Allyson. She provided her professional expertise in editing to give my book the final polish. She kept the book exactly the way I speak and the way I wanted to deliver it.

Third and finally is my wife, Chris. When I wrote this book and all the chapters, it was like putting a puzzle together to make it flow. She used her professional expertise to make this happen. She also designed the book cover which exemplifies the total chaos that surrounded my life and everyone around me during my addiction.

All three people had to endure reliving the darkest period of my life and accepted the challenge. I know for a fact, there were many times I would have to just stop and break away because of the bad memories. I'm sure it wasn't easy for any of them either, but I am truly appreciative of their commitment.

# Table of Contents

# Chapter 1: My Story

**This is the story of my journey since suffering a back injury on January 11th, 2001, and how, within a year of my injury, I was completely addicted to narcotics without even realizing it, until it was too late.**

Addiction comes in many forms. My addiction was with opioids prescribed to me as part of a "Pain Management" regimen following my injury.

I decided to write this book to share the last 20 years of my life. I hope that people who read this book will learn about the disease of addiction and seek help before it's too late.

In the beginning, I'll share a little about my life as it was before the injury and the many ways this injury turned my life and the lives of all those dear to me into a living hell over the next decade. This included my wife, children, extended family, and friends. Sometimes, my hell would fall at a complete stranger's feet at no fault of their own.

Pretty much everyone, at some time, has either known or knows someone suffering from some form of addiction, and probably most of you have known or know someone with opioid addiction.

I'll detail how my consumption of narcotics began and escalated through the years, all in the name of "Pain Management". How fast the quantity and potency of the prescribed narcotics increased, and the insanity of it all.

I will reveal how my addiction affected my relationships, sometimes nearly destroying them, and the mental and physical toll that addiction takes on others who share your life.

I will share my experiences with the struggles and determination that it takes for not only the addict to get clean but also how difficult it is for others around the addict. For me, the withdrawal process took over 2 years. I'll share the step-by-step process that I used to get completely off the drugs.

I'll describe how the drugs changed my physical appearance and personality, not in a good way. I'll relate stories of some of my unexplained, explosive outbursts and actions, mostly without me feeling any guilt.

My loved ones will share their thoughts, feelings, and experiences with me during my addiction and my road to recovery. When they provided their accounts, it was very tough, at times, for me just to read them. Not that I disagreed with what they had to say, but the difficulty was reliving the reality of the harm I inflicted upon them.

I will describe the day I had an epiphany and decided to accept the challenge of wanting to be drug-free as well as all the thought and preparation, mentally and physically, it took for such a challenge.

I will share the numerous surgeries I've had to endure since being clean, without being afforded any narcotic pain meds for relief during and after these procedures.

I'll tell you about my daily challenges and even, sometimes, the fear my family had to be subjected to, never knowing what mindset I might be in when they would return home. My wife even said she didn't know if I'd be alive when she got home from work, considering the incoherent state I'd be in after my daily doses of narcotics.

Now, after 10 years of sobriety, I've gotten most of my life back together. Unfortunately, during my addiction, I had hurt many, if not all, of my loved ones to the point where my actions or words left them scarred. The hurt I cast upon them was always mental and never physical. They've mostly forgiven me, but the scars will last a lifetime.

There were definitely times of trials and tribulations for myself and everyone around me during my addiction and withdrawal period, which lasted, in total, about 12 years.

Most importantly, I want to make sure that everyone understands that, at the moment I decided to get clean, I had the resources, support, faith, and love to be successful. I was blessed that I didn't wait to get off the drugs until the point of losing everything.

My book has been written to share the before, during, and after-effects that narcotics have on a person who becomes addicted. Hopefully, some of my writings will enlighten and give hope to people who are addicted and to the loved ones around the addict that their situation can change.

This change isn't an easy one, but as a 10-year recovering addict, the fight was well worth it.

So many times, during my addiction, I could have given up, or my loved ones could have given up on me, but neither they nor I did. Trust me, at times, I just wanted to end everything and stop the madness.

As you read, I hope you will find a few of the tools that helped me get to this point of my life valuable. I am now a drug-free person who has received a second chance at living and rebuilding relationships with the possibility of helping others with their addiction.

Please enjoy and learn from my story. For those who are suffering, "DON'T EVER GIVE UP!" The downside of giving up will only bring sadness, depression, destruction, loneliness, and eventually, a shortened and miserable existence, leading to death.

# Chapter 2: My Better Half

Until the infamous day of my injury, I was a very healthy 43-year-old man. I was employed, very active, happily married to Chris, who is English, and father to three young children. Brett was 16, Erica 13, and Bradley 7 years old. Chris is my second wife and the mother of Bradley. At that point, Chris and I had been married for 8 years. I'll share more about each of them later in the book as my journey continues.

First, I'll spend some time telling you all about Chris for many reasons, but primarily for being the catalyst behind my successful recovery.

I met Chris in March 1993 while she was visiting her childhood friend Tony, who had been transferred to the United States with his computer firm a few years earlier. The day I met her was a Friday, and I had been hanging out with some friends in Point Loma during the day.

At that time, I was living with my father, Keith, in the house that I grew up in, located in the San Carlos area of San Diego. I lived with my father because I had recently separated about 4 months earlier and was starting a divorce proceeding from my first wife.

After spending the afternoon with my friends, I decided to head back to my father's house, but not without stopping by a local bar to have a few beers. The bar's name was "Foggy's Notion" and was directly across the street from the San Diego Sports Arena. The Sports Arena was where everyone who grew up in San Diego went to see concerts, sporting events, the circus, roller derby, wrestling (real wrestling, haha), and everything else.

As I sat by myself at the bar at Foggy's watching some Basketball on the T.V., two girls and their male friend entered the bar. When they went to sit down, one of the girls sat next to me, and the other girl sat on the other side of her. The girl sitting next to me immediately introduced herself as Angela and starting to talk to me; she was a talker.

Angela introduced the other girl as Chris, who, at first, didn't say much to join in the conversation. The moment Chris did speak, I could tell she was British and had that funny accent.

As the night went on, the conversation between all of us never seemed to miss a beat. The guy they were with was eventually introduced as Tony.

When Tony and Angela decided to get up and do some dancing, that left Chris no option other than to talk to me one on one, and Boom, that's all it took. Chris and I talked for the rest of the night and even danced a bit ourselves. Being from two different countries, we were so different in every way that I found it so easy to talk to her.

As it turned out, Chris was leaving to go back to England that Sunday, so that gave me less than 2 days to get to know her better.

After much persuasion, I convinced Tony and Angela to let me give Chris a ride back to Tony's apartment. His apartment was very close to my father's house.

Chris and I got in my truck and left, arriving first to the apartment. I asked her if she could go out to dinner the next night before she left to go home to England. She said "Yes," but Tony wanted to go with us. He said he wanted to spend her last day in the States with her.

I'm sure he wanted to ensure Chris would be safe. I must say I was bummed out that Tony had to tag along.

Saturday evening came, and I went to pick up both Chris and Tony. We headed over to the Hotel Del on Coronado Island for some drinks, then to the Brigantine Restaurant for dinner. As it turned out, the evening was very enjoyable, even with the third wheel.

During dinner, I learned Chris was coming back to San Diego in July on a 6-month traveling visa. I was so pleased to hear that. Chris was the kind of girl I had never dated or hung out with before, and I really wanted to get to know her a lot more.

Sunday morning arrived, and it was time for Chris to go to the airport for a long journey home. Her direct flight was almost 14-hours from San Diego to London.

I went to pick her up at Tony's apartment. I was already feeling sad that I had only a little time to get to know her. When she answered the door, she greeted me with a friendly little hug and kiss, which picked up my spirits.

I bought her a bottle of Clos Du Bois Merlot to take with her. I then told her, "I would love to share it with you if you would allow me to come and see you in London."

Her face expressed excitement, but I knew what she was thinking, Yeah, right, he'll never make that journey; I just met him a few hours ago!

After Chris returned to England, we exchanged phone calls at least once a week. That was when long-distance calls abroad were still quite expensive. She made up for it by sending funny, cheerful greeting cards a couple of times a week. I always looked forward to checking the mailbox to see if another card had come.

About a month later, I made arrangements to go to England and see Chris. Traveling abroad was pretty easy for me. At the time, I worked at FedEx, and employees of FedEx had flying benefits. This benefit cost me only a few dollars for the 5,500-mile plane ride.

During my flight, I sat next to an older woman, and we started to chat. She asked me what was bringing me to England, and I went on to tell her about Chris and I meeting. She thought that was so nice and found it kind of romantic. She wished me luck and to have fun in her great country.

Upon arriving at Heathrow International airport bright and early the following morning and making my way through British customs, I met up again by chance with my elderly flying companion.

She asked if I had met up with my friend that I met in San Diego yet. I explained to her that I actually took an earlier flight than I had scheduled. This flight had arrived in London about an hour earlier than the flight I told Chris. She suggested that I go over to the Passenger Service Kiosk and have Chris paged over the intercom to meet up with me.

So off I went to do just that. I started to tell the Service Agent that I would like to have a person paged. The agent said, "no problem, what's her name?" At that moment, I was like a deer in headlights and somewhat embarrassed, realizing I didn't even know Chris's last name.

The agent didn't seem fazed, and she went to make the announcement for Chris over the intercom, saying, "Can Chris, who is meeting Greg from San Diego, please come down to the Passenger Service Kiosk to meet him?" As I waited at the kiosk, I wasn't only feeling embarrassed but also ashamed and disappointed for not knowing her last name.

As it turned out, Chris was already at the airport waiting for the scheduled flight that I told her. She was having a coffee right above me on the next level. Within a few minutes after the announcement, Chris met me at the kiosk. How nice it was to see her and hug her again.

We finally got to her car as we proceeded through the airport parking garage, and I tried to get into her driver's side door, completely forgetting the English drive on the WRONG side of the road. When I looked over at Chris, she was already laughing.

As we drove in her little Peugeot back to her flat (apartment) in the North Finchley area of London, I was in awe just taking it all in. It was like everything I had imagined. The design of the buildings and houses looked like they were straight out of the "Mary Poppins" movie.

Once we arrived at her flat, I was immediately introduced to her Collie mixed-breed puppy named Shadow, who went by the name Shaddy, we instantly bonded, and he quickly trained me to take him on walks!

Her flat was 2 stories, fairly large, and pretty impressive. It was an old Victorian building with a long deep narrow garden (backyard).

You would think at this point, all I would want to do was sleep, especially after the long flight with absolutely no sleep. But my anxiety was so high that I couldn't wait to go out and explore London, especially having a true Londoner as my personal tour guide.

As soon as I was unpacked, we headed out and drove to the local tube station (underground train) to head into the center of London and start taking in the sights.

During the day, we would duck into a pub to grab a pint, something we did a few times throughout the day. I loved the pubs; they were a blast.

Learning the ins and outs of riding the tube and jumping on and off the red double-decker buses to navigate through London was quite an experience. The public transportation in London is the best way to get through the city because the traffic is horrendous, and it will take you forever to get anywhere if you drive.

As the first day of sightseeing ended, we returned to her flat. On the way back, we decided to stop by Blockbuster Video to pick up a VHS video. You remember Blockbuster Video and the VHS, right?

After the long day, we just wanted to go back and relax and watch a movie. The movie we picked was "My Cousin Vinny," and we also grabbed a pint of Haagen-Dazs chocolate ice cream.

Once we settled on the couch and began to watch the movie, Chris pulled out the bottle of Merlot that I gave her to take back to England when she left San Diego. We sat there drinking the wine, eating ice cream, and watching the movie.

To this day, "My Cousin Vinny" has a special place in our hearts.

This trip to England was only for a weekend arriving Friday and leaving on Monday.

A few months later, in May, I decided to go back to England for another weekend trip. That meant that I traveled to England twice in less than 2 months for short weekend stays.

That equates to over 22,000 air miles, and I probably would have flown over again if Chris didn't already have plans to come back to the United States.

Chris came back in July, and I met her at the airport. She was a welcome sight for sore eyes, even though it had only been 2 months since we saw each other.

Back in 1993, you could go to the actual gate to meet your visitors. Wow, how things have changed since then.

I took her back to Tony's apartment, where she would be living for the next 6 months, and let her get settled in.

During the next 6 months, we would date and hang out, but we would still do our own thing. I was getting out of a failed marriage, and the last thing I wanted was to get into another steady relationship right away.

As the months went on, we started to do most things together. Chris was getting to really know Brett and Erica, my children from my previous marriage. Brett and Erica were 7 and 4 years old and became comfortable with Chris and enjoyed being around her. I think they could tell I was happy being with her.

Shortly after Chris arrived in July, Erica asked me, "When is your friend going home?" but it didn't take long for Erica's feelings to change and do a complete 180-degree turnaround. She loved hanging out with Chris and gave her the nickname "Kidda."

Chris's visa was ending in January of 1994, and she would be required to return to England. She wouldn't be allowed to return to the United States without waiting at least a year before being allowed to return on another Travel Visa. I didn't want to see her go, even if it were for only a year or so, and neither did Brett and Erica.

Everyone who came to know Chris soon felt the same way; they didn't want her to leave.

"Oh, she's so good for you."

"Oh, you guys are so good together."

I think everyone was more caring of her than me; just kidding!

After spending 4 or 5 months hanging out with Chris, I really got to know her. I enjoyed being with her; I could feel myself seriously starting to fall for her. Even though I tried to fight those feelings, I couldn't help myself.

There was never any drama with her. After these months, I knew she wasn't the type of girl who was out to try and change me or mold me into someone I wasn't.

In late November of 1993, after much serious thought and consideration, I decided to ask her to marry me. To my surprise and without any hesitation, she said "yes," and the wedding plans began.

Choosing a date for our wedding, Chris thought it would be nice if we married exactly a year from the date that we met on March 19th. I agreed, and we made wedding plans for March 19th, 1994, on the Bahia Belle on Mission Bay in San Diego. The Bahia Belle is a 2-story paddlewheel boat with a top deck.

The invites were sent out, and the guests from England and elsewhere made their travel plans.

Since her visa was expiring in January, 2 months before our planned wedding, she contacted the INS (Immigration and Naturalization Service) to seek an extension.

The INS informed her she couldn't get an extension and that she would have to leave the United States, return to England, and wait 6 months before she could apply for another visa.

Ouch, now what do we do? We'd made the reservations, paid deposits, and guests had made travel plans. Everyone from England and across the country had already bought their airfares, booked hotels, and sorted out all the other logistics that go along with a wedding.

After much discussion, I decided Chris and I should go to Las Vegas alone, not telling anyone, and just get married. Las Vegas offered a wedding package that included transportation to the courthouse to get the marriage license, transportation to the Candlelight Wedding Chapel for the ceremony, and then transport back to the Desert Inn Resort where we would be staying.

On the evening of December 17th, 1993, we left for Las Vegas and our secret wedding. I still remember the look on Chris's face once we came over the hill and saw the Las Vegas Strip's lights. She was like, "wow!"

The following day, Saturday, December 18th, as we prepared for our secret wedding, I became so nervous that I couldn't even tie my tie! I had to go downstairs to the concierge and have him assist me.

I also had this sick feeling in my stomach that I hadn't told anyone what Chris and I were up to.

After getting my tie sorted out, I decided to give my sister Vicki a call and let her know what was about to take place. It was before everyone had cell phones back then, so I had to go to a phone booth.

I made the call, and she was so excited for the two of us. I could also tell in her voice she was also a bit disappointed that we didn't let them know. She said they would have loved to be with us on this special day, but she said she understood.

We were picked up in a limousine from our hotel early in the afternoon. We were driven to the Clarke County Courthouse to apply for the marriage license. Chris was dressed in a cream knee-length dress - she looked beautiful - and I was in a suit.

Upon arriving at the courthouse, there was a line of other couples waiting to apply for their licenses. Some of the brides standing in line were in full-length white wedding gowns and long streaming veils. Kind of funny to see if you were there.

Once the marriage license was issued, the limo driver drove us over to the wedding chapel for the ceremony.

The minister who greeted us appeared to be a bit intoxicated and had already started his drinking for the day. We weren't sure he'd be able to stand through the vows!

The minister asked us where our witnesses were? Chris and I must have missed this memo. He suggested we go out to the Strip and ask some random strangers to be our witnesses.

Seeing a bride and groom out on the Las Vegas Strip looking for witnesses must have been quite a sight. It sounds strange, but it was, after all, Las Vegas! We found witnesses, and the ceremony proceeded; Chris and I were officially married.

Our marriage is a testament of time because neither the Candlelight Wedding Chapel nor the Desert Inn Resort are still in existence.

We still had our originally planned wedding on the Bahia Belle on March 19th, 1994. Again, nobody knew other than my sister and brother-in-law that we went to Las Vegas three months earlier and tied the knot, only to avoid the deportation requirement of her Travel Visa.

The March wedding was also very special for both Chris and me. Chris had all her family and friends there from the U.K., and I had all my family and friends there too. The big exception was my mother's absence, who had passed many years prior. My mother sure would have loved Chris, and it's a shame they never got to meet.

Once the boat left the dock the ceremony pretty much started. We completed our vows for the second time, and the party started, and it was quite the party.

We provided an open bar with only the best booze, music, and dinner. By the end of the night, both families and all our friends had become one big family. Everybody was talking to everybody, really making connections, and having a great time.

After roughly 7 years of marriage, I convinced Chris to apply to become a U.S. citizen. She completed her citizenship application at the beginning of 2000. Nearly 2 years later, she was notified to appear for an immigration interview, which I was required to attend with her. Within 2 months of the interview, Chris was granted her U.S. citizenship. America is lucky to have her as a citizen

# Chapter 3: My Children

Let me briefly share a little information about my kids because I can't understate how much support all three of them provided me, not only during my addiction but every day since.

Brett graduated from San Diego State University in 2011. He went on to work for an online university, where he met his wife, Allyson. Brett and Allyson were married in October 2017 in the La Jolla area of San Diego. Brett has since switched careers and gone on to be a radio producer for the San Diego Padres, the San Diego State Aztecs Basketball and football teams, and KIIS FM-L.A. Currently, he is an Executive Producer for PodcastOne in Beverly Hills. He and Allyson relocated to Sierra Madre, a suburb of Los Angeles, and Allyson continues to work for an online University.

Erica graduated from Azusa Pacific in 2015 and works in Medical Administration. She was married to Jonatan in February 2019 at the Welk Resort in Escondido, a city about 25 miles north of San Diego. Jonatan also works in Medical Administration. They purchased a home with lots of land in Santee, CA, in November of 2019. They have three dogs, and their large lot is perfect for the dogs to run around and play on.

Bradley graduated from Sonoma State University in 2016 and is currently serving in the United States Air Force. He married Maddison (Maddie), his High School sweetheart, in October of 2020 at the Glider Port in La Jolla, just a bit south of Torrey Pines Golf Course. Their original plan was for a large wedding with 200 guests, but this had to be changed due to the COVID situation and restrictions, and it ended up being immediate family only. Brad deployed to the Middle East in January of 2020, returned safely in August of 2020, and is currently stationed in Charleston,

South Carolina. Brad and Maddie have a lovely apartment in Mt. Pleasant, about 30 minutes from his base. Maddie still works for the company she worked for in San Diego, but now she works remotely from Mt. Pleasant.

As you can tell, I have been truly blessed to have three great kids with college degrees and fantastic spouses. Chris and the kids are true blessings, and I can honestly say, if it hadn't been for them, I would have never survived the journey I'm about to tell you.

So many people contributed to and are responsible for my success in sobriety and my survival. Chris is the one who took the brunt of my pain, aggravation, hostility, and craziness, but the kids, Brett, Erica, and Brad, were next on the totem pole.

My sister and brother-in-law, Vicki and David, their daughters Amber and Ashley, and, of course, my father Keith were always there for support, love, and comfort.

Throughout the book, they'll be sharing individually the experiences they had to go through with me and my addiction. Everything they share will be put in the book exactly how they wrote it. I'll also share my feelings about each of them later on.

# Chapter 4: My Loved Ones

I dedicate this chapter to my loved ones who had to live with me and experience all the pain and mental anguish I was going through, as well as the pain I subjected them to.

I asked my immediate family to write a short piece for me to be included in my book. They've written explaining their experiences and feelings toward me during the 10 years of my addiction.

This was the first time I had heard a lot of their comments. Obviously, they were too afraid to express their feelings at the time, fearing how I would react. I didn't have a very good track record when hearing something I disagreed with.

During my time of addiction, my personality changed significantly. I had become a person who could and would explosively react to pretty much anything at any time. Now that I have a clearer thought process, and I remember some of my explosive altercations with my family, I realize they only had good intentions for my health and wellbeing at the time, along with the health and wellbeing of everyone around me.

Some will share the love they had for me and, at other times, the disdain and sometimes downright hatred they had toward me for what I had become.

Often, the disdain and hatred they felt I brought upon myself for the way I acted, spoke to, and treated people. Unfortunately, I took my frustration over the never-ending pain that I was experiencing out on my loved ones.

For some strange reason, I thought my behavior and how I would treat people at times was acceptable and that they should understand.

Over time, their tolerance for my behavior wore thin, and some made decisions to limit their interactions with me. Limiting their interaction wasn't an option for Chris or Brad, who lived with me 24/7.

Chris and Brad's only escape from my persona was work for Chris and school for Brad. Trust me, neither one of them were in a hurry to come home. When they came home, I'm sure they were scared to some degree, not knowing what kind of mood I was going to be in.

That wasn't an environment that any wife or young child should have been subjected to. This, by no means, is to minimize the tension and fear my other loved ones had to experience.

Unlike Chris and Brad, the other family members could live their lives in some degree of normalcy because they could block me out of their thoughts if they weren't around me. However, they didn't completely abandon me because of the unconditional love and support they offered.

My whole family has been raised not to turn your back on family. These morals are deeply ingrained and have been demonstrated by each of them at one point or another. I can honestly say if it hadn't been for this quality that every member of my family showed, I wouldn't be alive today.

Even after 10 years of sobriety, I still sense that, at times, they have some doubts about my trustworthiness, integrity, and choices and decisions.

As the years go by, I feel like their doubts are slowly fading, and my previous relationships with each of them are improving and being rebuilt. The following few chapters include their stories precisely printed the way each one was written.

# Chapter 5: A Letter from My Eldest Son, Brett

I remember my dad being Superman. I remember him flying through the air in Mission Bay as he backflipped off of a floating dock into the water below him. I remember his physical strength: lifting, carrying, and moving things with the least bit of effort. He could throw a baseball harder than anyone I knew. I remember his ability to read people and get the best out of them. Most importantly, my dad had this uncanny ability to sense when others needed help. He would always show up and save the day.

When I was a kid, my dad worked as a beer distributor, a mailman, and a FedEx courier. Like Superman, whatever the task entailed, he suited up and delivered. As I grew up, I realized that was a common theme in my dad's actions: he showed up, and he delivered. Whether it was coaching Little League games, helping with Boy Scout projects, or teaching me how to drive a car, he showed up, he delivered. He had an identity. My dad knew who he was to his family, his friends, and to the world. He knew what was needed of him, even when we didn't, and he always rose to the occasion. When he encountered an obstacle, he faced it and overcame it. He protected those who needed protecting and defended what he knew was right for him and for the ones he loved.

Then he broke his back and his tailbone, and Superman was brought to his knees by pain no one should endure.

I'll never forget the next decade, not because my father proved again how he could overcome any obstacle, but because he finally lost. A "doctor" prescribed him Vicodin, Oxycontin, Soma, and other medications I had never heard of before.

Medicine is supposed to be good for you, and we trusted those meds that ruined the next ten years of our lives.

As the medications increased, my father faded. Instead of taking off and backflipping into a pool, he would "take off" in a different way. We'd have my dad for an hour or two before he was drifting off, washing away into a place of oblivious comfort. He'd become mentally and socially absent but able to tolerate the pain. We didn't like this reaction, this "medical treatment," but it made the pain somewhat bearable for him. We didn't understand the dark place the meds would take him. His moods would swing between anger, frustration, and justifiable self-pity. He started breaking down the ones he cared about, seemingly without notice. Whether it was my stepmom, my sister, my brother, other family members, friends, or complete strangers, we all faced that darkness in one way or another.

We tried to act normal, carrying on with holidays, dinners, baseball, and softball games. We convinced ourselves life was still normal. We went on trips to take him out of his routine, hoping to find the person he was before the meds. But then the fights began. Whether it was at a family gathering, an amusement park, a restaurant, or a hotel room in Florida, he would get in our faces. He wouldn't back down. He became belligerent, eager to fight as if it helped him avoid fading away. My dad didn't care whom he hurt or who was watching, and my stepmother often had to physically stand between him and his new enemy.

Fights and altercations seemed more worth it to him, and, like the meds, he continued to dig deeper and deeper. At first, I thought he was addicted to the destruction. But then I realized it was the medications, how they seemed to put him in a bubble. And still, we continued trying to convince ourselves that it's just medicine. How can it be wrong?

The meds pushed us out. We feigned normalcy while my dad continued to fade. I never knew what was going to set him off. Happy moments became rare as he fell apart.

He and I started to see each other less and less. I think in avoiding him, I was avoiding a mixture of fear and sadness. Fear of how awful the situation had become. The overwhelming sadness of having to watch my Superman throw us away. I started college and tried to find other things to focus on. For years, I "wouldn't be able to make it" for dinners, for weekends, and for trips.

My fear and sadness manifested into pure resentment. For what he became. For his apathy. I didn't matter anymore; our family didn't matter anymore. When we did see each other, I told him how I really felt. I thought, If I fight, he'll know I care, and if he knows I care, he'll know I love him.

I'll admit now that I struggled to show compassion. I wanted to hurt him. I'd call him pathetic. I wanted to take my pain out on this man who was already at his lowest. I needed to pay him back for all that he did to me, to us. Just like I thought he was doing, I wanted to burn it all down, the good and the bad. I wanted to start over.

But still, I couldn't forget the person he once was, Superman. And my dad and I both realized that we were never going to give up on him.

Palm Springs, 2009, he told us for the last time that he was going to quit. And for the first time in almost eight years, I believed him. With a sad dread in his eyes, he seemed to finally recognize the damage that had been done and the journey he had ahead to salvage the broken pieces. I was cautious, but I finally saw that first glimmer of light so far down this dark tunnel. The dark tunnel we all had been traveling down with him. I realized that my dad needed to recover when he was ready to. It was going to be tough, for him, for all of us, but more than ever, he knew that we were all in it for the long haul. He hadn't lost any of us, and we were going to be there for him, whether he wanted it or not.

He went through hell to get off the meds. The loss of sleep, the constant sweats, the mood swings; it was clear that these drugs were fighting to stay a part of his life, just as we were. In a dark irony, these drugs reacted similarly to how I reacted as I felt my dad was "quitting" us. They fought viciously to remain.

Eventually, his smile came back. He began to enjoy things with a sober mindset, one not fogged by Somas, Oxycontin, and Vicodin. He became far less volatile. He started to help again: giving his family solid advice, donating his now clean blood to those who needed it, volunteering for church, and finally returning to the world he belonged in and could improve.

Deep down, I knew he always cared for us, but he started to express these feelings more often to his family and friends. His ability to read people and know what they truly needed, whether it was a hand, a hug, or just someone in their corner, was back. He wasn't backflipping or lifting things like he once did. He had a different strength to show now, a new strength I grew to respect, love, and admire more than what I once looked up to as a child, one that still makes me think of one name, Superman.

***Dad, I thank God we have you back.***

---

Brett is the oldest of my three children and has the biggest heart in the world. Even though Brett and I have never really discussed the effects of his mother and I divorcing when he was only 7 years old, considering his "heart of gold," I'm sure the divorce really took a toll on his childhood in many ways.

For a few years prior to the divorce, I was very involved in Brett's sports, most of the time being a coach. If I wasn't coaching him, I was in the stands being his number-one fan.

After the divorce, the ability to continue being a coach for his sports was taken away from me. I changed careers and went to work for FedEx and my new schedule impacted the time it took to be a dedicated coach. I tried to make it to most of his games and continued to cheer him on.

After my injury, I knew our relationship had withered over time. Everything he has written about me is true and I can't take any of it back. I knew in my heart he had these feelings of resentment toward me, but I never really wanted to accept them.

The visitation schedule for Brett and Erica was pretty much standard for most California divorces involving kids. I would have them every Thursday night and every other weekend along with switching major holidays every year.

For almost 11 years of following the visitation schedule and until Brett turned 18, there were only a couple of times that I was unable to fulfill this schedule.

As the years went on with my "Pain Management," I began to sink deeper into the darkness of my drug habit. Brett started to give excuses to opt out of some of the visitations, which irritated me, but I knew in my heart the real reason why.

As far as the annual vacations that Chris always insisted on, there may have been just one trip that Brett didn't go on, and that was just a conflict of schedules. Brett knew before these trips that they held the potential for me having a "meltdown" over something stupid, which would cause him embarrassment, fear, or pain, or the trifecta of all three, but he still went with us.

Even before my injury, I didn't consider myself "Father of the Year." A little story that Brett will never forget is when we went to San Diego Chargers football games.

A group of my friends all had season tickets for the Chargers, and we would gather in the same spot in the stadium parking lot hours before the start of the game. We would eat, drink, and have lots of laughs. Great times!

When it was time to enter the Stadium for the game, I would smuggle a few beers in, so I didn't have to pay the outrageous prices for the Stadium's stale, flat, and disgusting beer.

This is how the beer smuggling operation went. I would take my binoculars out of their case and hang them around my neck. I would put 4 beers into the empty binocular case, hang the case with the beers around Brett's neck and walk right past the security guards. Definitely not a good example for a father to set for his son, but Brett and I have laughed about this memory numerous times over the years.

When Brett was in high school, he was a member of the drama program. A few of the plays Brett performed in were *Snoopy* and *The Little Shop of Horrors,* along with others. Loving to perform, Brett and a few of the other drama members started an improv comedy show that they performed every other month.

When his performances were on the calendar, it gave me something to look forward to. I knew after each show I would be coming away with a big smile on my face from the laughter of the performances, especially the improv gigs. The performances were spontaneous and really bought out the member's individual talents…and Brett would always hit a home run!

There is one thing Brett said to me during my addiction, and I've never forgotten it because it brought me to a new low spot in our relationship at the time. He said, "Dad, when I talk to you on the phone, you always seem to be preoccupied, and I feel like you could care less about talking with me."

I took his comment and gave it some serious thought, only to realize he was right. It wasn't that I could care less about talking to him; it was the fact that when we were talking, I wasn't really paying attention to what he was saying.

From that point on, every time we speak, I make every effort to give him my undivided attention and listen to every word he has to say.

That one statement made me aspire to be a better person because I knew Brett wasn't the only person I would blow off and not listen to when talking on the phone.

Now that I live in Florida, I get out to San Diego to see everyone at least every three months. Seeing the kids and their spouses is a priority and always one of the first things to get on the schedule, and for as many times as possible. The quality time spent during these visits is fantastic and always enjoyable, and the visits are only getting better.

I feel like our relationship is the best it has ever been for both of us. Words cannot express how grateful I am that you didn't give up on me and have allowed me to always be in your life. I'm genuinely thankful that you found such a great wife as Allyson to share your life with.

**Love you, Brett and Allyson!**

# Chapter 6: My FedEx Courier Position

First, let me explain my position at FedEx. I was a courier and absolutely loved my job. My schedule consisted of working Monday through Thursday.

I would start my workday around 6:00 am, and the day would end anywhere from 6:00 pm to 7:30 pm.

Shortly after arriving at work, I would conduct a vehicle inspection on the van, truck, or Grumman, whichever would be required to make a run to the airport to pick up the first overnight freight that needed to be delivered to the recipient before 8:00 am.

After completing the first overnight deliveries and returning to the FedEx Station, I would go to another vehicle that I would be using for the route that I would be on for the day.

I was called a "Floating Courier," and I considered it to be the best position at FedEx. Some couriers worked 5 days a week and others only 4 days a week. Those who worked 5 days a week worked an 8 to 5 Monday through Friday schedule. The ones who worked 4 days a week had the same schedule as I had - 6:00 am till whenever that day's outbound freight was off to the airport, generally around 7:00 pm.

Floating courier meant I would cover a particular courier's day off, a courier who had a 4-day workweek. So, every Monday, I would be running the same route, every Tuesday running the same route, and the same for Wednesday and Thursday.

Let me tell you a little something about the routes I had. On Monday, my route would start in Jamul and end up in Jacumba. This route didn't have a lot of deliveries (generally between 35 to

45 stops), but it had a lot of driving, sometimes over three hundred miles for the day. This route wasn't very physically demanding but could be mentally challenging.

This was a very rural route in the mountains of San Diego County, and most of the delivery recipients lived well off the beaten path away from anyone else.

First, I would find their mailbox, located on whatever the closest paved road might be. Then I would have to decide which dirt road I would proceed on. Sometimes, I chose correctly; other times, I didn't.

The recipient's home could be several miles down this dirt road. While driving down the dirt road, I wouldn't see any houses or structures and sometimes wondered if I'd made the wrong choice.

I would look for electrical power lines, knowing they supplied power to something. Once I located the house or structure, I would go to the door and try to get an answer.

If no one was there, and if the package was allowed to be left (without a signature), I always wanted to ensure I was at the correct location. Many of the homes located out in the middle of nowhere don't have house numbers.

I would have to look for something with an address on it. Most of the time, that meant looking through their trash for something with an address on it, such as a piece of junk mail.

Once I was sure I was at the right place and left the package, I would never forget how to get there.

This route ran along Highway 94 along the U.S./Mexican border, and I would frequently see illegal immigrant activities along with several Border Patrol checkpoints.

I have a funny story about something that happened to me on that route during the Christmas season. That's when the package volume increased significantly, and FedEx would have to rent additional vehicles to get the increased volume delivered.

On this particular day, I was in a yellow Hertz high cube truck. I had to go to a house with a backyard property line that backed onto the U.S./Mexican border.

After driving miles down this rolling black asphalt road and then onto the dirt road that led to the house, I was met by the homeowner who was anxiously waiting for his package. We had a short but friendly conversation about him being a retired Border Patrol officer.

As I headed back down his dirt road and got back onto the asphalt road, I came over one of the little hills and was met by two Border Patrol agents. They had their weapons pulled and pointed at me. They instructed me to get out of the vehicle with my hands above my head.

Once I was out of the vehicle, they immediately recognized my FedEx uniform but still weren't convinced I was employed with FedEx. They both approached me, still armed, but guns lowered a bit and asked me to open the roller door on the Hertz rental truck.

I walked toward the back and slowly opened the roll-up door as the agents stood there prepared, not knowing what they might find.

At this point of my route, it was near the end of my day, and I had only a few packages left to be delivered.

Once the agents were satisfied that I was who I said I was, we all had a little laugh. They explained that these types of rental vehicles are commonly used to smuggle drugs and illegal immigrants into the United States.

As I mentioned earlier, this route might take up to 300 miles of driving, and, often, I would be driving on dirt roads for 150 miles of that. There were only 3 or 4 couriers at FedEx who knew how to run this route

This was also at a time when cell phones were just becoming available. Even if you had a cell phone, there was no signal/reception due to the mountainous terrain. So that limited trying to call the recipient for directions to their home.

I would be in the San Diego State University area for my Tuesday route. This route had houses, apartment buildings, businesses, and parts of the college. It was also a busy route with lots of deliveries and pickups. This area had a high density, and parking was a challenge.

Chris (my wife) would meet me sometimes for lunch on this route because she worked not too far away.

This route was pretty much uneventful other than me hustling and running most of the day. As it turned out, the Tuesday route would be the last one I was ever on for FedEx because of my injury.

Wednesday was an interesting route that consisted of the "Mile of Cars" area of National City. This area was 95% car dealerships and businesses and required driving the Grumman's largest delivery vehicle in the FedEx fleet.

The Grumman would be completely filled with parcel packages, car parts, and FedEx letters and envelopes, several hundred of them. The thing about this route was that most of those deliveries would be required to be delivered by 10:30 am, FedEx's Priority Service.

My deliveries were generally finished by noon, allowing me to take a long lunch of 2 hours. Quite often, I would eat my lunch and get in the back of the Grumman to take a nap before I started the pickup cycle of my day.

Since this route was made up almost entirely of businesses on a typical day, I could have up to over 120 stops for delivery and pickup.

When I first began doing this route, I was preparing my packages in the back of my truck at the FedEx station before heading out to start the deliveries. I began to catch the smell of pot (marijuana) in the back of the truck where the packages were being put into delivery order. The smell was becoming stronger and more pungent, and I was thinking, "*Man, somebody is shipping a shitload of pot!*"

I decided to inform my manager of the smell, and when he came over, he just started to laugh uncontrollably. He then told me that the smell was coming from packages going to be delivered to the DEA (Drug Enforcement Agency) Laboratory for testing.

When the DEA confiscates drugs from illegal activities, the drugs are sent off to the DEA Lab to test potency and quantity.

I soon learned to make the DEA Lab stop the last stop of my "Priority" deliveries. The DEA protocol for receiving evidence deliveries is for one dedicated individual to be responsible for receiving these types of deliveries.

This individual would inspect every package separately to ensure the box hadn't been tampered with. This delivery might be in 10 separate packages or more, and it always took some time to verify that they hadn't been tampered with. The receiving person would never sign for the delivery until the inspection process was completed. The person's name would have to be entered into the tracker by 10:30am in order to have proof of delivery before the commitment time.

The area this route covered was very small and compact, allowing me to deliver up to 30 stops in an hour and maybe 15 to 20 pickups an hour. Pickups always took a longer time to complete because of the paperwork. Sometimes, the shipments weren't always ready to be shipped, even though the shipper would say they were prepared at a particular time.

My Thursday route, which was a rural route in the mountains with lots of driving and maybe 35 to 45 deliveries and pickups, started in the town of Alpine and ended up at the U.S. Air Force Radar Station on the top of Mount Laguna. The highlight of this route was the view to the east overlooking the deserts of Southern California, including El Centro and Borrego Springs. What a beautiful view it was.

One of the time-consuming stops would be to pick up fake ammunition that would be used in the movie/television industry. Boy, did I hate having to go out to that place!

Sometimes I would have to go out there to make a delivery and then go out there again for a pickup. Going out there twice would take up to 1 ½ to 2 hours alone—a real time-eater.

As I mentioned earlier, my work schedule at FedEx consisted roughly of 12-hour days Monday through Thursday, starting around 6:00 am to after 6:00 pm. It's amazing how fast a 12-hour workday goes by when you're continuously moving. Also, having a 4-day work week allowed me to have three-day weekends with Friday, Saturday, and Sunday off every week. That was so nice!

With this schedule, I would start my work week with a mild delivery and pickup day but lots of driving. Not much sleep was required the night before. I would have to hustle on Tuesday and Wednesdays and then have another mild delivery day on Thursdays, but again with lots of driving. God, I wish I were still doing this for a living, but, unfortunately, that wasn’t in the cards.

# Chapter 7: My Injury

So now, with a better understanding of my job, let me explain how my injury occurred on January 11th, 2001, in Descanso, California, while I was working for FedEx.

This is where my nearly 10 years of drug addiction - in the name of "pain management" - and treatment plan begins.

I was on my Thursday route from Alpine to Mount Laguna when I suffered my career-ending injury during a bizarre snowstorm in Descanso.

It was a cold, stormy day with blizzard conditions (believe it or not, considering San Diego's climate), and the snow had started to really drop fast.

I made a delivery that required driving up a long steep, asphalt driveway. The trip up the driveway was successful, but when it came time to return down the driveway, the weather conditions had severely worsened, and the black asphalt was frozen and iced. To make matters worse, the homeowner had parked his new Range Rover at the bottom of the driveway in anticipation of the bad weather.

I knew if I decided to drive back down the driveway, I would most likely be unable to control the FedEx vehicle, and it would start sliding uncontrollably and most likely take out the parked new Range Rover.

After consulting with FedEx dispatch, the decision was made to send out another vehicle and transfer all the freight into a new vehicle, leaving the first vehicle behind until the weather improved and the first vehicle could safely be retrieved.

The freight had to be loaded onto a hand truck/dolly and wheeled down the frozen driveway to transfer the freight from the stranded vehicle to the new vehicle.

I successfully made the trip down the driveway twice, but unfortunately, the hand truck went to slip on the third trip, and then I slipped and fell onto my butt.

With the freezing weather, I didn't feel anything except for the jarring hit my buttocks and spine took from the frozen ground. As the day continued, I started feeling pain and discomfort, thinking I possibly bruised my tailbone.

Once the freight was transferred into the replacement van, I became the passenger and let my coworker drive. Within minutes of going down the curvy iced road, the van skidded off the road and into a shallow ditch. My coworker and I were able to free the van from the ditch and continue making the remaining deliveries.

Since my injury occurred on a Thursday, I had the next three days off. I thought I would have the long weekend to feel better and improve. When Monday came around, my condition hadn't improved, but I was able to work with much pain and discomfort.

When Tuesday came, I went to work as usual and did my deliveries, still with the pain and discomfort as the day before. I was hoping to just make it through the day.

As I was making my pickups late in the afternoon, all of a sudden, my legs didn't want to work correctly, and I became really concerned about what was happening with them.

I notified FedEx of my situation, and they asked if I was able to drive back to the station or if I needed someone to come and get me. I was able to drive back myself, and upon my return to the station, I was told by management that I needed to go for some medical attention.

Since it was late in the evening, I said I would go to the doctor's first thing in the morning. That was unless my condition got so severe, then I would go immediately to the Emergency Room at the hospital. I made it through the night without worsening and went to the doctor bright and early the next day.

# Chapter 8: FedEx Mandated Treatment

When you have a work-related injury at FedEx, you're required to seek treatment from a physician contracted with the company. Unfortunately, with these "company contracted physicians," I believe their primary goal is to minimize the injury when possible and get you back to work ASAP, which means going without the necessary testing to identify the injury and the source of the pain most of the time.

Taking these shortcuts minimizes the expense for treatment and doesn't get the patient the care required to make a complete recovery; it just puts the patient in a position for another injury or worsens the current injury.

**I will refer to all of my doctors using fictitious names to protect myself and them from any legal ramifications.**

The first physician I saw was the company doctor named "Dr. Dumb-Dumb." At first, he seemed genuinely concerned and interested in getting my injury diagnosed and starting a treatment plan. Dr. Dumb-Dumb started with what's known as a "Conservative Treatment Plan," which consisted of X-Rays, anti-inflammatories, and some basic pain medication.

After a month or so of the conservative treatment plan with NO improvement and my condition worsening, Dr. Dumb-Dumb suggested another approach. He prescribed a series of three epidural injections.

These injections were performed by "Dr. Butthead" and were executed at various surgery centers throughout San Diego.

After the second injection, I developed the worst headache of my life and conveyed this to Dr. Butthead. His response was that these headaches were common and would go away in a short time. He instructed me to increase the pain medication until the headache went away. Well, the headache didn't go away and wouldn't go away no matter what I tried to do.

I completed the series of three injections over 7 days, and still NO improvement for my back pain, and the raging headache continued with no relief and no concern from the doctor. Dr. Butthead's only comment was, "Give the epidurals some time to work."

After a couple more weeks, Dr. Dumb-Dumb told me that sometimes, it takes a few series of epidural injections to alleviate the pain and suggested I get another batch of three epidurals from Dr. Butthead.

I agreed to another series, but I complained relentlessly about my constant, debilitating headache to the doctors. However, they weren't concerned by this in the slightest.

After starting the second round of injections, I began to find it strange that every appointment with Dr. Butthead would be scheduled at a different surgery center location. I questioned Dr. Butthead about this and why he couldn't do the injection at the exact location each time. His explanation was, "It has to do with the surgical center's schedule, and I can't do anything about it." It sounded reasonable to me at the time, and I accepted his explanation.

It wasn't until arriving early one day at the parking garage for an appointment that my father and I saw Dr. Butthead arrive and park his car. We watched in amazement as he unloaded the trunk of his car with all sorts of supplies and thought this was very strange.

After completing the whole second round of injections and still not showing any signs of improvement and experiencing the worst headache, I decided it was time to switch doctors and get a second opinion for my treatment and care.

After a certain amount of time, a "Workmen's Compensation" patient can opt-out of the treatment they're receiving from the dictated insurance doctor. The patient can seek treatment from a doctor of their choice. Upon learning this, I started to review some new options and spoke to a few other people who had some similar experience in dealing with Workmen's Compensation.

I spoke with a coworker who had been involved in a horrific FedEx big-rig accident where he nearly lost his life. I shared my disappointment with him about how my treatment wasn't progressing well and the lack of improvement. He suggested I go to a doctor who treated him after his crash.

He also suggested that I get legal representation specializing in workplace injuries to protect myself, my right to proper medical care and treatment, and my future livelihood.

Getting concerned that I may never get rid of this headache and back pain, I decided to go with the doctor who treated him. The doctor's name was Dr. Steven, and I made an appointment for the first opening he had. My appointment was scheduled within a couple of days.

During my appointment, I learned Dr. Steven had some experience and knowledge about the cause of my headaches. He suggested that I see an anesthesiologist.

My immediate thought was I'd been seeing an anesthesiologist (Dr. Butthead) for nearly 2 months, and his treatment had done absolutely nothing to treat my back pain or the headaches.

Dr. Steven assured me the anesthesiologist he was referring to had plenty of experience with patients experiencing these types of headaches. As it turned out, my headaches were caused by a "spinal leak." Just these words gave me some hope that at least he knew the cause, and I could get relief from the headaches.

From that moment on, Dr. Dumb-Dumb and Dr. Butthead were in my rearview mirror and were never to be seen by me again.

I made an appointment with the new anesthesiologist. Within moments of meeting with the new anesthesiologist, he immediately diagnosed the cause and knew how to eliminate my "spinal leak" headache. The doctor explained to me that an "epidural blood-patch" procedure would rid me of my headaches, and he scheduled the procedure ASAP.

"An epidural blood patch is a surgical procedure that uses autologous (same individual) blood to close one or many holes in the dura mater of the spinal cord, usually as a result of a previous lumbar puncture. The procedure can be used to relieve post-dural puncture headaches caused by a lumbar puncture (epidural injection). A small amount of blood is injected into the epidural space near the site of the original puncture, and the resulting blood clot then "patches" the meningeal leak."

My 2-month-long extreme headache was caused when Dr. Butthead performed the second injection in the initial series of injections.

Apparently, when Dr. Butthead was locating where to place the epidural injection into the spine, he missed his target and had to try again. The missed attempt caused a puncture in my spinal dura mater (spinal cord casing), from which the spinal fluid leaked, causing a severe headache.

"This type of spinal leak causes the spine to contract and cause "intracranial hypotension." Other symptoms of spinal leaks can be, nausea, vomiting, neck pain and stiffness, hearing problems, imbalance, and sensitivity to light."

Immediately after my blood patch was performed, my headache was gone for good. I couldn't believe how long I had suffered because of Dr. Butthead's negligence and how quickly the headache went away with the simple blood patch.

I actually cried in the car with Chris after getting the blood patch procedure because I no longer suffered from the debilitating headache. I couldn't believe I had suffered for so long when there was a such an easy remedy.

Dr. Butthead could have performed the blood-patch procedure, but to do so, he would have had to admit to making the puncture in the first place when performing the epidural and accept fault. Plus, he would be held financially liable to correct it without reimbursement from the insurance company.

Thinking it was strange that Dr. Butthead wouldn't acknowledge his error and remembering how he had to provide all his own supplies for his cases, I decided to do some research on the good old Dr. Butthead.

Much to my surprise, I found that Dr. Butthead had had his medical license and hospital privileges suspended or revoked more than once.

I also found out why he had to provide his own medical supplies for all the procedures he performed. It was because he would use the surgical center supplies and not pay for them. The facilities stopped him from using their inventory. Kind of like dining and dashing!

Believe it or not, Dr. Butthead is still practicing medicine today!

I cannot emphasize enough how important it is to conduct your own due diligence and research your doctor's history, qualifications, and license status if you have a serious illness or injury. Do your research to find answers to the following questions:

Are they in good standing with your State's medical board?

Have they ever been reprimanded?

Have they ever had their license revoked or suspended?

Unfortunately for me, I didn't do my "due diligence," and I ultimately paid the price for it. Not only did I suffer longer than needed with the headache, but the original conservative treatment plan with Dr. Dumb-Dumb turned out to be more conservative and not aggressive enough.

When Dr. Steven became my attending physician, treatment became more aggressive, efficient, and attentive. Dr. Steven immediately got me scheduled with an MRI and other required testing to obtain a thorough diagnosis.

After the MRI was completed and reviewed by the neurosurgeon, it was determined that several of my spinal discs and vertebrae were damaged. The bulging of the discs was pinching the nerves, causing all the pain I was experiencing.

The problem for me was the fact that I had numerous levels of my spine that were damaged and needed attention. Prioritizing which level of the spine to address first to give me some relief was the primary goal.

In the meantime, FedEx's lawyers decided to take me to task. Before they would approve any kind of surgery or treatment, I would have to be subjected to many additional procedures such as myelogram, discogram, and electromyography.

The **discogram** is very barbaric. The anesthesiologist inserts a needle through the spine and into the disc. After the needle has been placed into the disc, pressure is applied by inserting a sterile liquid through the needle, causing pressure on the disc. If the disc is damaged, the patient will immediately be in excruciating pain to the point of tears. By documenting the severity of the pain, it is determined how damaged the disc is.

"The **electromyography** is where small needles are inserted through the skin on your thighs and into the muscle then given an electric shock to detect any neuromuscular abnormalities."

Not much fun getting poked with needles and waiting to get shocked.

After completing all of the required testing, it was determined I needed a "spinal fusion." Not a single-level fusion, but a 2-level fusion from L2-L4.

At the time, a 2-level fusion didn't have a high success rate, but for the extremely damaged condition my spine was in, it was my only option.

## My First Surgery

My spinal fusion surgery was scheduled for September 12th, 2001, at Mercy Hospital in San Diego. The surgery was estimated to take around 8 hours to perform, and I would stay in the hospital for about 7 days to recover.

On the morning of September 11th, while I was mentally trying to prepare for my surgery the following morning, the United States experienced the 911 Terror Attacks. Like everyone else, I didn't know if America was at war or what was going on. After much talk with the surgeons and hospital, it was decided to proceed with the scheduled surgery as planned.

A lot was going on in my mind. Kind of scary knowing I'd be stuck in a hospital with no mobility if the attacks were the beginning of a war.

On Tuesday morning, September 12th, I was required to be at the hospital by 5:00 am. Upon my arrival, I was registered and prepped for surgery.

This was the hardest time for me, waiting to be carted off to the OR (operating room). When I was finally carted off, I couldn't help wondering if I would make it through an 8-hour surgery and if this would be the last time I was going to see my wife and family. I think everyone who goes through surgery has the same thoughts.

As I was wheeled into the OR, the surgery assistants were preparing all the surgical tools that were needed while rocking out to the booming music of Led Zeppelin. The music was actually quite comforting.

Before I knew it, I was under sedation, and the surgery was on. When the sedation cocktail was inserted into my IV, they asked me to count backward from 100, but I didn't even get to 95 before I was out! The last feeling I had before going under was the coolness of the sedation going up my arm.

Dr. Arthur performed my first spinal surgery, and it took roughly 8 ½ hours to complete. I made it through without any complications, and the professionals considered it a real success.

The procedure included the removal of what was left of my 2 discs between levels L2 and L4, and the insertion of cadaver bone along with titanium hardware rods and bolts.

In 2001, this type of surgery required cutting through my muscle mass and nerves, with an approximately 8-inch incision. The surgical tools used during these surgeries were still pretty brutal. These tools included power drills, saws, even a hammer, and a chisel. I'm sure they all have proper medical names, but they're the same tools found around the house.

The recovery time for this surgery was estimated to take almost 18 months for me to get as good as I was going to get.

After waking up in the recovery room and then returning to my hospital room, I had never experienced the amount of pain I had before, and that's with all the pain medication I already had in me.

The good old Morphine drip was the best relief option, but you can only push that button so often as it's a measured and timed dose. You can press the button as many times as you want, but if it's not time for the scheduled dose, there is NO drug available.

The physical therapist came in the next day after surgery to get me up and get my body moving again. On the first day with the therapist, I had to walk the hospital halls with my I.V. pole in tow.

The next day, the therapist had me go to the staircase and climb a flight of stairs. The I.V. pole became my best friend and provided the pain juice that allowed me to do these little tasks. After I completed my daily physical therapy, I was utterly exhausted.

The hospital room that I was in for the next week was on a higher floor and had a fantastic view to the west toward the bay and the Pacific Ocean.

For the first few days, I had a roommate who was dealing with kidney stones and the pain associated with that. After he was discharged, I had the room to myself, which was nice. I didn't have to worry about watching T.V. or how loud it was. I also didn't have to worry about the strange noises I would make due to the pain. There was a lot of moaning and groaning!

When I was finally discharged from the hospital and returned home, the pain was so severe that a "pain management regimen" was initiated.

# Chapter 9: The Ups and Downs of Physical Therapy

The first pain medicine that was prescribed for my pain was Vicodin. With any kind of movement, the pain would be almost unbearable. For example, just wanting to roll onto my other side while lying down was probably the hardest thing I had to do. It was something I had to do, and I knew what the price would be for doing it: pain, pain, and more pain.

One side effect that I've experienced after every surgery is the feeling of being nauseated nonstop. It appears to be caused by the hours of anesthesia and the sedation cocktail used (I call it poison). This sickening feeling was no fun when it was added to the extreme pain that I was already experiencing. Enough is enough!

I was prescribed a medication called Ondansetron which is given to cancer patients to help reduce the feeling of nausea when receiving chemotherapy. It didn't really help me. The thing that helped me the most for the nausea was a product called "Cola Syrup," which can be purchased over the counter. It's the Cola syrup used in soda fountains like those used in a fast-food restaurant such as McDonald's or Burger King. The syrup is heavy and thick and definitely provided relief for my nausea.

My first big outing was my sister-in-law's wedding just 10 days after surgery. It wasn't much fun for me, considering the pain, but at least I was there to share the big event with her. The Hawaiian-themed wedding was held in their backyard and had a large number of guests in attendance. They even had a pig roasting in a firepit, which was a first for me! That's where I found out that a pig's testicles were an appetizer - not for me, thank you.

A concern that I had was that I didn't want to be the center of attention and wanted to keep the focus on the bride and groom. I was able to get situated and seated before most of the guests arrived, so my condition was pretty much under the radar for the ceremony. The wedding was a success, and everyone seemed to have a have a great time celebrating, including myself.

As it turned out, all I needed was a little Vicodin and a few beers to tolerate my pain. Since I was new to taking Vicodin, I didn't know then that narcotics and alcohol are a dangerous mixture and can cause accidental death by overdose.

I was required to wear a shell brace around my back and chest to limit my mobility, so I wouldn't damage any of the work that was done during the surgery. I soon learned how to protect myself from being vulnerable to incidents. This meant I looked and made sure of every step I took so I wouldn't trip or fall. I also learned how to position myself when I was out and about to minimize the risk of getting bumped into.

A few months after the first surgery, I decided to go and watch my son Brad's soccer game. As I stood on the sideline away from absolutely everyone, one of the players from the other team chased a ball that went out of bounds and ran straight into me. I might as well have been hit by a dump truck for the amount of pain this caused. That was the end of my outing for the day, and I had to immediately return home to recover.

About a month after surgery, I started a physical therapy (PT) program. This program consisted of riding a stationary bike, massage, heat, ice, and a TIMs stimulating unit. I was instructed to go three days a week for therapy for the foreseeable future.

Once I arrived at the PT Facility and got checked in at the front desk, the receptionist let the therapist know I was there. The therapist would get me started on the stationary bike, and I would ride for 15 minutes. After my bike ride, the therapist would continue with the other rehab therapies.

One day, I went to PT, as usual, checked in, and started riding the bike. After several minutes of riding, the bike's seat post either broke or wasn't totally in a locked position. This caused the seat, with me on it, to drop about 15 inches and come to an abrupt stop. At that point, I thought I was going to die from the pain this sudden fall caused. I was also really scared that this fall may have damaged the work that was performed during my surgery.

A call was made to my wife to inform her of what had happened and ask her to come and pick me up.

As soon as I got back home, I called Dr. Steven and was able to talk to him. He instructed me to get to his office as quickly as possible for an examination. Once Chris and I got to his office, we talked about what had happened, and he ordered a series of X-rays.

I went to the radiologist and had the X-rays completed and directly returned to Dr. Steven's office so he and I could review them. When he looked at the film, he discovered I had suffered a broken/dislocated coccyx (tailbone) from the fall. The pain I was experiencing was like having a sharp object stabbing you in the ass and tailbone. Ouch!

Dr. Steven was confident he could get this fixed right then and there. He described how it had to be done and that had me frightened. He started by saying he would insert his finger up my rectum, locate the coccyx, and pull on it to adjust it back into the correct position.

He insisted my wife be in the room at the time of the adjustment. I think it was so she could share in my trauma. Just kidding; I think it was for his protection too.

After the bike accident, I never returned to that PT facility again.

A couple of months after the coccyx adjustment, I was able to return to therapy at a new PT facility. It also meant that I would have to start at ground zero again regarding the therapy rehabilitation. That's when Dr. Steven really went to bat for me.

Dr. Steven insisted that FedEx, their lawyers, and their insurance agree to send me to Frog's Fitness Center for aqua therapy for the remainder of my PT, lasting almost 6 months.

The therapy at Frog's was much more professional and very intense. The therapist was always there upon my arrival to make sure I was physically prepared.

My routine would start by riding a stationary bike for 15 minutes after the therapist inspected it to ensure it was in proper working condition. That was never done at the previous PT facility. Then I would do a circuit of weight machines lasting around 20-25 minutes, starting with minimal weight and minimal movement and steadily increasing both over time.

Once I completed the indoor routine of bike riding and weights, I would proceed to the outdoor pool. The pool exercises were the most challenging and most demanding part of therapy.

I would put on floating ankle wraps along with a floating vest and get into the pool. The floaties would immediately want to pull my legs out from underneath me and flip me over. The purpose of these floating devices was to make me fight this urge and build up my core muscles.

I'm sure it was pretty comical at the beginning for anyone watching me flopping around in the water like a fish that had been hooked and was trying to get released. It took some time and a lot of sweat to master this. It soon became easier and easier, but then the therapist would introduce new maneuvers and exercises that demanded even more strength and determination to complete. I bet you didn't think you could sweat in a pool, but I was proof that you can.

After returning home from a PT session, I would be totally worn out and in a lot of pain. When I was in the water, my body joints decompressed, allowing me to have more movement and flexibility, but the pressure would return to joints with more intensity when I exited the pool.

After a few months of aqua therapy, I must say I was in the best shape of my life. I was pleased and proud of myself, but it took a lot of hard work and a lot of pain to get to that point.

As my treatment got more intense and the costs escalated rapidly, FedEx and their attorneys were trying to find some kind of mitigating factor to minimize their liability. They hired a private investigator (PI) to follow and videotape me, trying to catch me doing something I shouldn't be able to do, considering my injury.

The PI would follow me to Frog's Fitness Center and try to gain entrance to observe me doing my indoor bike and weight routine, but he was denied entry because he wasn't a club member. He still watched me through the fence when I was in the pool doing my PT thing.

On one occasion, the PI thought he had caught me in the act. Unfortunately for him, he was actually recording a friend of mine playing basketball in front of my house.

His declaration was "it was Greg shooting the basketball" when anyone could clearly see it wasn't me. Not even close to looking like me. Eventually, the PI had to admit he was wrong.

Another time, the PI sneaked around to the back of my house beyond my property in an open area. He was again hoping to catch me doing something, but who knows what?

While he was spying on me in my backyard, I had to make a trip to the store. When he realized I was leaving, he ran back to his truck to try and catch up with me. He had no idea I knew he was watching me.

Since I was just going to the grocery store, I allowed him to catch up to me. He didn't know where I was going. He stayed pretty close behind me in the right lane as I was driving in the left lane. At the very last moment, I pulled into the turn lane to enter the shopping center.

My decision to turn was too late for him, and he couldn't change lanes in time, so he had to continue to go straight. I parked and watched him make the first turn he could and drive through the parking lot looking for me. I have to say; I got a good laugh watching him scramble.

The PI had no success and struck out twice in the attempts that I witnessed. His expense was a complete waste of money for the insurance company. I learned over time that the insurance company would rather spend 10 times the amount of money to try and minimize their liability than to provide the proper care and treatment needed to recover from an injury.

# Chapter 10: Life After FedEx

Since my first surgery in 2001 severely restricted my ability and hopes to return to FedEx in my normal capacity, I had some life-altering decisions to make.

What if I didn't return to FedEx? What would I do for work? My options were limited because my entire working career had been a very physical one. Now those strengths were no longer with me or had seriously been diminished.

Now I was basically a stay-at-home dad, spending quality time with the kids.

I was able to attend the kids' school functions that I couldn't make prior to my injury. These activities included field trips, school plays, school sporting events such as track and field day, and even the dreaded parent-teacher conferences.

When Brad was in second grade, his class went on a field trip to ride on a buckboard pulled by horses to tour a farm. The opportunity arose for me to go along with the kids and the teacher to help chaperone. The field trip was scheduled for just 2 months after my first back surgery. I thought this would be a good chance for me to get some fresh air considering I had been housebound pretty much since my surgery.

Brad and I arrived at his school the day of the field trip, and I met all the other parents going along with the kids. The problem was, all the other 6 parent chaperones were mothers, no fathers.

My first thought was, *Oh no*. Not that I have a problem with mothers, but I was thinking this might be a long day listening to them share their war stories.

I wasn't totally disappointed because Brad's second grade teacher was a man. I kind of thought he was thinking the same as I was: Oh boy, what's the gossip du jour going to be?

At the time, I must have been one of the first stay-at-home dads, and I didn't like having that thought. To me, it was kind of insulting to my pride and manhood. Nowadays, stay-at-home dads are very common, and I don't think it has the stigma that it did once.

Another brilliant idea of mine during this time was to go out and buy a new Yamaha 450cc street motorcycle.

Being in the mental and physical condition I was in at the time, taking 16 narcotic tablets a day, pretty much having a numb left leg, and not having all my faculties, what could possibly go wrong?

I would give Brad rides to and from school and rides to and from his sports practices.

On my own, I would travel down the freeway at high speeds, take long winding rides through the mountains, and even take rides at night, all under the influence of narcotics.

Once in a long while, I would make a good decision. One of those decisions was to park my motorcycle in the garage permanently.

After I parked the motorcycle and reflected a bit on what I had done on it before it was parked, I felt blessed that nothing had happened to me or anyone else. I must have had a Guardian Angel looking after me, considering the potential disasters that could have occurred while riding.

The cause of my numb/dead left leg was a signal that another spinal disc was going out. This would eventually lead to my subsequent surgery in 2007 - more on this later in the book. Hey, lucky me!

Being a stay-at-home dad allowed me a lot of free time to think about my future career.

I had always been interested in Real Estate, especially with the home prices in California, so I decided to study and apply for a California Real Estate Salesperson License.

I successfully studied and passed the California Real Estate Exam and became a licensed real estate agent in 2002.

After studying and passing the exam, I became even more interested in the real estate business and wanted to learn everything possible to be successful.

Shortly after acquiring my RE License, I had to decide if I wanted to stay with FedEx. If I chose to stay with them, it would have to be in a different capacity.

Staying with FedEx would most likely be me taking an office position, and I had never had an "office" job. FedEx offered me a position processing the paperwork for international packages at a reduced salary, and I seriously considered it but ultimately decided not to accept the position.

Chris and I made the choice to part ways with FedEx and get some additional training applicable to my real estate license.

My thinking was, "now is my chance to start a new profession," and one that I already had studied, completed, and obtained a license for.

FedEx offered me some financial assistance toward retraining which I accepted. They paid for my tuition so that I could get the certification for Mortgage Financing. Not only would this education benefit my real estate career, but it would also be another revenue stream for me.

I've always enjoyed finance, not to the point of sitting in an office and crushing numbers, but to know the financial needs of potential homebuyers and homeowners who want to refinance, so I enrolled in a mortgage and finance course. The course came naturally to me, and I loved the challenge of calculating people's qualifications when trying to purchase or refinance a home, finding their debt to income ratio (DTI), their loan to value ratio (LTV), and reducing their debt to qualify for a mortgage, etc.

One of my best traits is the ability to talk to just about anyone and feel comfortable doing so.

I had a good run in the real estate and mortgage business for almost 2 years, and then BOOM! My back required another level to be fused, and so in June of 2004, I went under the knife again and all the rehabilitation time that goes with it.

Now, going through another 18 months of rehab so close to completing my first rehab period was a major blow to my mental state.

The second surgery began a very dark period for me because I was really starting to feel sorry for myself.

I felt self-pity because of all I'd been through, taking opiates every day, not being the person I used to be physically and mentally, and having deteriorating relationships with family and friends. I was becoming an emotional wreck.

It got to the point when Chris left for work, I would walk her out, watch her drive off down the road, and then start to weep. It became so bad that Chris wouldn't know if I would be dead or alive when she got home.

During this dark period, I attempted to return to my Real Estate & Mortgage business. One of the best blessings during this time was when my friend Jeff Schmidt wanted to explore the possibility of purchasing a new home.

Jeff and his family had lived in Mira Mesa for over 30 years, and now that all the kids were grown up and had moved out, he and his wife wanted to see what options were out there.

I met Jeff when I was 18 years old and joined his recreational softball team known as the "Crabs." Jeff and I immediately became good friends and have continued that friendship for over 40 years. If I were in real trouble and only had one phone call to make, the call would be to him.

Jeff and his wife wanted to escape life in suburbia and go rural. Since their desirable properties were in the undeveloped area of San Diego County, Jeff always offered to drive his big Ford F-350, 4-wheel drive truck to view potential properties. This worked out well because most of the properties he wanted to view were generally down a washboard, bumpy road or even worse.

The most difficult chore for me was getting in and out of his big-ass truck. During nearly the next 2 years and after viewing over a hundred listings, the Schmidt's found their perfect dream home in Ramona.

Ironically, their new home is located on the same road where many of my relatives owned land in the 1960s. As a kid, my family and I would go up to their properties and ride dirt bikes, shoot guns, and I even learned how to shoot a bow and arrow there.

These trips were tremendously helpful to my mental health during the 2 years of looking, and I don't think Jeff realizes how therapeutic they were to me. At this point in time, I was at the lowest and deepest point of my addiction and under the most potent influence from opiates.

It got me outside for most of the day, which was a novelty for me at this point, and we would always stop for lunch. Most of the time, our lunch was at "The Boll Weevil" restaurant. Other times it might be at a local casino on one of the many nearby Indian reservations.

I don't think Jeff ever realized how much these days out meant to me.

**Thank you so much, Jeff!**

Jeff and his wife and my other 99% of clients were great, but I also dealt with the polar opposite type. I sold the home of one of my clients when they moved away from San Diego. When returning to San Diego, they asked me to assist them in finding a new house.

The wife would fly into town from New York, leaving her husband at home to continue to work. She and I would spend the next few days checking out potential homes. The problem was she didn't really know what she or her husband wanted. So, my task of finding them a new home was a difficult one.

One day, she would want to look at the biggest house possible; the next day, we would be looking at a tiny beach house. The day after that, it would have to be a newer home, and then it would be a fixer-upper. You get the picture.

When the husband was able to fly out with her, the criteria would change again. The challenge was that we could never go out to view listings until the Ohio State Football game was over. Then I would have to take them out to lunch or at least a Starbucks before heading out to view their listings of the day.

I worked with them for almost a year, trying to find them a suitable home. The husband soon joined her in the indecisiveness, and the situation became very frustrating for me. We finally came to a mutual agreement to part ways without ever finding them a new home to purchase.

This was another major mental defeat for me, and something I've never gotten over. The amount of lost time, the amount of money, and all the effort on my part that was seriously wasted.

**If they read this book, they'll know who I'm talking about.**

# Chapter 11: My First Vacation Post Surgery

Now it's time to move on to some of my trials and tribulations while being an active drug addict.

While recovering from my first surgery, there was a lot of adjusting that occurred so that I could function somewhat normally. I had to learn how to maneuver everything all over again, getting in and out of bed, going up and downstairs, getting in and out of a car, tying my shoes, getting in and out of a chair, and all the other movements you do throughout the day. I had to retrain my brain and body to do everything a new way.

One of the most significant reality checks was realizing I would never be the same. Most of my strengths, both physical and mental, had now become weaknesses, and the sooner I accepted that, the better off I'd be. Easier said than done. This new mindset was depressing and very demoralizing for me.

In the spring of 2002, about 6 months after my first surgery, Chris, Brad, and I went on a road trip to San Francisco. Erica was planning on going with us, but she and her mother decided that she wouldn't be going the morning we were leaving. I was disappointed, to say the least, but I think Brad was more upset. Brad really loves his sister and was looking forward to the trip with her.

At that time, we had a Volkswagen Eurovan, which had a bench seat, table, TV, and rear-facing seats. The kids loved playing games at the table or watching a movie while on road trips. With the Eurovan, getting in and out was easy compared to getting in and out of a sedan, and it had much more room in it to stretch out.

This was my first getaway since the surgery and I really didn't know what to expect or how I would do.

Chris booked a brand-new hotel in San Francisco called the Argonaut for a week. It was located right on Fisherman's Wharf. The trip ended up being fantastic and tremendously helpful to my mental health, along with Chris and Brad's.

I'll never forget on our way back to San Diego, we stopped by Universal Studios in Los Angeles to catch up with some of Chris's friends from England.

We had booked a Sheraton hotel, and when we arrived, we required some assistance with our bags. That's where we met the bellman who helped us with our luggage. He was an older, very tall, and strong-looking gentleman.

While he was bending over, unloading the cases out of the back of the van, his shirt raised above his waist, and I saw a scar identical to one I now had from the surgery. I asked him about his scar, and he told me all about the surgery he had many years earlier.

Listening to the description of his surgery, it seemed very similar to the one I just had with only one exception; his surgery was only a one-level fusion compared to mine being a 2-level fusion. My take-away from our conversation was there is hope for me; look how he lifts and moves these suitcases around. That was nearly 20 years ago, and I remember it like it was yesterday. He became my inspiration.

Even at the beginning of my drug use, it didn't take long for my demeanor to change and even my whole personality. I no longer had much patience and often had unexplained outbursts. It's just the nature of the beast when you become an addict.

Chris had always insisted on taking an annual vacation to some destination. Brett and Erica were always invited to join our yearly vacations, and most of the time, they would, but sometimes, there was a conflict in schedules, and they wouldn't be able to go.

Over time, it seemed like they had more and more scheduling conflicts so that it would be just Chris, Brad, and me.

I think Brett and Erica were acutely aware that the potential existed for me to have a meltdown or confrontation at any moment about anything. They knew I didn't care, and I didn't care who witnessed it, so chose not to go. Brad's good friend Chad came along with us on a few trips when Brett and Erica didn't go. Chad was never a problem and he provided Brad with some company other than just Chris and me. Hanging with mom and dad could get boring, demanding, and overwhelming.

When I was younger, I frequently went on vacation to Lake Tahoe to go skiing, hiking, or just to play in the water, which is generally chilly because the lake water is mostly melted snow. One of the good things about Lake Tahoe is after you've enjoyed your day doing outdoor activities, you could go out and enjoy the nightlife at one of the many casinos there.

Here's a little story about one of my many trips there before my injury:

One of my trips to Lake Tahoe was with 15 family members and friends to go skiing. After spending the day on the slopes, we all enjoyed the evening gambling. I wasn't having much luck at the tables that night and decided to return to the hotel. As I was crossing the 2-lane highway that runs through South Lake Tahoe, I pulled what remaining cash I had left out of my pocket and dropped one of the paper bills onto the street.

As I immediately stopped, turned around, and bent over to pick up the bill, a car's bumper went right past my head, narrowly missing me. The driver of that car thought I had passed his path and had no idea I was going to suddenly stop, therefore barely missing me. The bill I dropped was only a dollar, and I almost lost my life over it! Another reminder of how you could lose your life in an instant.

In May of 2004, Chris, Brad, and I went to Lake Tahoe and stayed at The Ridge in South Lake Tahoe near Stateline. Lake Tahoe is beautiful every season of the year. The summers are warm and perfect for watersports, and the winters are a hotbed for snow skiing, with ski resorts dotted all around the lake.

I tried so hard to participate in some of the activities and adventures the place had to offer but was restricted by the condition of my health. I remember Chris and Brad would go play racquetball, and Brad would go shoot hoops. We would take drives around the lake, and we went for a paddle boat ride on the lake.

One day we decided to go the lake beachfront to relax and watch Brad play in the water.

The beach we went to offered parasailing, and Brad really wanted to give it a go. When we inquired about booking it, we were informed that Brad wasn't heavy enough to go solo. The only option for Brad to go was for Chris or me to go with him.

The choice of which one of us would accompany Brad wasn't a tough one because Chris was an immediate "Oh hell no!"

So, it came down to me as the only option to go with Brad. I was in no physical shape or condition to be pulled by a tow line to a high attitude with Brad attached to me, but since I felt like I had already lost the ability to be a good father, I accepted the challenge and agreed to fly with him.

After we took off and reached our altitude, the sky was absolutely clear, and the water below was so crystal blue that the thrill of the ride kicked in. During our flight, I pointed out landmarks that I had learned from my previous trip to Lake Tahoe, such as ski resorts with their still snow-capped mountain peaks and other famous points of interest on the lake, such as Emerald Bay.

After our wonderful flight, we landed back on the beach and continued to enjoy the rest of the day.

When we returned to the Lodge that evening, I decided to take a shower. While washing my hair and rinsing, I felt a sunburn on the top of my head that I had never felt before. It really hurt. After getting out of the shower, I looked in the mirror to see how bad the burn was and realized for the first time that I was losing my hair. I had always had a full head of hair and never imagined I would start to go bald, even though I did start going gray when I was about 16. The gray hair used to come in handy when I was young because I was one of the few who could go and buy beer!

Throughout the rest of our stay, my pain continued to worsen. I knew the kind of pain I was having wasn't anything good, and over the next couple of days, the pain became so bad I was in tears. At this point, we decided to head back home, which was an 11-hour road trip, and I was in no position to drive.

At that moment, I didn't realize that this trip would be one of my highlights for the next several years. The pain, mainly in my left leg, was so bad it felt like my leg was broken in two, and the two "broken" bones were rubbing against each other, causing unbearable pain.

We started the more than 500-mile drive home with Chris at the wheel of our Honda Passport SUV. As I lay down on the back row of the Passport, I couldn't for the life of me get into a position that would relieve my pain.

I would get comfortable for a moment or two, but then the sharp tearing of the muscles, bone rubbing against bone pain would rear its ugly head and bring me to tears. Even with the narcotics, I had little to no relief from the pain.

Can you imagine yourself being on a drive for over 500 miles with a young boy as your co-pilot and a whining, crying, grown man in the back seat, and there was nothing you could do to ease my pain or shorten the drive?

Chris was the real hero on this mission to get home, driving all the way, only stopping once to refuel and grab some fast food. After making the 10+ drive home, I was in so much pain that I couldn't tolerate it anymore. As soon as we got home, we dropped Brad with his grandparents and headed straight to Sharp Memorial Hospital to seek help.

Upon arriving and being admitted to the emergency room, the ER physician was at a loss of what to do, so he injected me with a large dose of Morphine. The injection gave a little relief, but not much. As the doctor continued to identify the cause of my pain and discussed my previous back surgery, he concluded that he couldn't help me any further. He felt the best plan of attack was to hit me again with another dose of Morphine, instruct me to make an appointment with my surgeon ASAP and then send me on my way. Then, right before I was discharged from the emergency room, he decided to inject me with a third dose of Morphine. That made a total of three shots of morphine within an hour and a half, and man, I felt like I was parasailing once again, having an out of body experience.

On the way back home after leaving the hospital, I became so nauseous from the Morphine to the point that Chris had to pull the car over to the side of the road so I could vomit, and boy did I vomit. I could still taste the Morphine that was oozing out of the inside of my cheeks and in my mouth. It's a taste that I'll remember for a lifetime.

After clearing my stomach of everything on the side of the road, we continued to head home. By now, it was about 3 am, and Chris had had enough drama for the day, so when passing the neighborhood elementary school on the way home and approaching the 3-way stop sign, she just blew straight through the sign without hesitation! It had to be one of the worst days for

Chris, as it consisted of making the 10+ hour drive from Tahoe, which wasn't the easiest of drives, then spending the wee hours of the morning in the emergency room waiting for me to be treated.

# Chapter 12: A Letter from My Daughter Erica

My father had an addiction, and because of his addiction, it created great affliction. I grew up resenting my father not only for the pain he caused me but the empty feeling he left in my heart. I know this wasn't the person he was raised to be and especially not the person he wanted to become, but years of drug dependency created a person that no one could relate to or even wanted to be around.

Lately, he has done his best to make amends for the deep scars he has inflicted on me and our family. Sometimes I wonder if it is too little too late, but at the end of the day, all I want is to be close to my father and have a good relationship with him.

These days I feel like I'm learning who he is all over again. I love who he is now and feel like we can finally move past our differences and learn to love each other for who we actually are instead of what his addiction made of us.

Erica

---

Unfortunately for Erica, her memories of me being her father and living in the same house are very limited due to her young age at the time of the divorce.

After the divorce was finalized, there was animosity toward me from Brett and Erica's mother and her family. Most of the animosity came from how quickly I had met Chris and got on with my life.

Erica was 4 at the time, a very impressionable age, and it's my opinion that she was sometimes used as a pawn to get back at me. When this happened, it always caused a lot of tension, not only between Erica and me, but for many other family members on both sides. I don't want to sound like I'm berating her mother or her family, but I think kids are often used as pawns during and after a divorce, which is sad.

Fortunately, I have lots of great memories of Erica when she was young, and I've always taken care to be the best father possible.

When Chris and I bought a house in the Scripps Ranch area of San Diego, we would have Erica and Brett every Thursday night and had to get them to school early Friday morning. At the time, they went to two different schools that had two different start times. I would drop off Brett at his school and take Erica to my father's house until her school start time. One of our favorite memories was hanging out at grandpa's house, where she always had peanut butter toast and chocolate milk for breakfast.

When we took them back to their mother after a weekend stay, Erica would always have to have a bowl of mint chocolate-chip ice cream. The funny thing was, she never wanted to eat it until we were in the car and driving back to her house.

I would like to share a story about something extraordinary and scary that happened to Erica when she was a baby.

When Erica was only about 2 months old, her mother laid her down for an afternoon nap in her crib. After a short time, I went to look in on her, and her appearance didn't look normal, almost comatose. I tried to get her to react to my touches, but she was unresponsive.

I instantly decided to rush her to the hospital, which was only 5 minutes from our house. Her mother didn't react with the same urgency but agreed it was best to go and have her checked out.

Upon arrival at the emergency room, Erica was immediately taken back to a room for diagnosis by a very young doctor. This young doctor made an immediate request for a spinal tap.

Scared to death and not really knowing if this doctor knew what he was doing, we decided to proceed with the spinal tap. The minute the spinal fluid was withdrawn, he knew that the fluid didn't look right and had the sample rushed off to the lab for diagnosis. Within minutes, the sample results were back, and it was determined that Erica had spinal meningitis.

She was immediately checked into the hospital, put in a private room, and put into a medically induced coma to reduce the swelling of her brain.

For the next few days, her condition was touch and go. Erica ended up staying in the hospital for a week. For that week, I never left her side, spending the nights in the room with her. I wouldn't have had it any other way.

From that moment on, I felt we had a special bond. She has always had a special place in my heart, and I realize just how lucky we are to still have her with us.

Thank God!

Chris and I always took an annual vacation with all the kids, but as the years went by, Erica's participation became less and less frequent. On more than one occasion, she would back out of a trip at the very last moment, and I mean the very last moment. For example, we would be planning to leave at 9:00 in the morning, and we would get a call at 8:30am saying "she wasn't feeling well" or some other lame excuse. This was disappointing to Chris and me and to her brothers, especially Brad, who totally idolizes her. Brad could never understand how or why this would happen.

Now for Erica's biggest disappointment in me. First, let me explain that I love all three of my kids the same, with my whole heart, not one more than the other, but all the same. I've always tried to illustrate this to them, and hopefully, they all understand, but sometimes emotions run high and make it feel that that's not the case.

In February of 2019, there was a massive scheduling conflict. Brad, Erica's younger brother, was graduating from the United States Airforce Bootcamp in San Antonio, TX, on the very same day as her wedding rehearsal dinner in San Diego. What are the chances? I didn't want to miss either of them.

I explained my predicament to Erica, hoping she would understand my decision to attend both Brad's graduation and then her wedding the next day, which meant missing the rehearsal dinner.

Our plan was to fly to San Antonio on Thursday to share Brad's graduation with him on Friday morning and then fly out to San Diego Friday evening. With the timing of these two special events so close to each other, there was no way I would be able to attend the rehearsal dinner back in San Diego.

Once we were checked into the hotel where the wedding was taking place, I immediately reached out to Erica to let her know that we were there and that we were really looking forward to the wedding. She insisted on me going over to her room to see her, and I did. It appeared everything was good, and excitement was in the air. We chatted for a bit, and then I returned to my room.

The wedding the next day was a great success. Erica was so beautiful, and I delivered my "father of the bride" speech without a hitch.

At that point, I thought I had successfully attended both once-in-a-lifetime events, with the only exception of missing the rehearsal dinner. Apparently, I was completely wrong and would only find out a few years later.

I found out through a friend how devastated Erica was with me missing the rehearsal dinner. It turns out that Erica's aunt shared

Erica's feelings with a good friend of mine, knowing it would get back to me, with the sole purpose of making me feel worse than I already did.

At that time, I was unsure if Erica's husband Jonatan knew the whole story about my addiction. The topic hasn't ever come up in the years since. His lack of knowledge about my addiction probably falls in the category of "my dirty little secret."

Just a few months ago, out of the blue, Erica called me and was a little emotional. The reason for her call was to tell me how she feels about me now. She went on to say how much she loves me and appreciates all that I've done for her, how I never missed visitation time with her and her brother Brett.

Erica, I love you more than anything, and I feel our relationship is better now than any other point in our lives. Thank you for sticking around and not giving up on me!

**Love you, Erica and Jonatan!**

# Chapter 13: A Few Perks of Chris's Job

In 2003, Chris started working as a Creative Director for a resort company, which gave her the benefit of booking timeshares pretty much anytime she wanted to.

We would go several times a year to a Marriott, Hilton, or other property for a week and sometimes longer. Being in the business, she was able to book these fantastic properties at a ridiculously low price. What a perk!

These little trips would be all over the country. Some of the resorts we stayed at were in Palm Springs, Lake Tahoe, Las Vegas, Virginia, North Carolina, New York, and many in Florida.

Palm Springs was always a favorite for everyone. It was only a short 2-hour drive from San Diego. Sometimes, Chris would book 2 or 3 units at the same time so family and friends could come and stay comfortably. We always had a great time.

On several occasions, Chris and the kids would come out and stay 3 or 4 days, and when they left to go home, my buddies would come and hang out for the remainder of the stay.

On one trip, Chris booked villas in Orlando for 2 weeks. Chris's good friend from England and her family met us there.

My birthday is on September 17th, and Chris would always book a timeshare stay for my birthday. Most of the time, it would be at one of the properties in Palm Desert, a town just east of Palm Springs.

Chris had another great perk with her job: getting tickets to special events. Most of these would be sporting events. Her company did a tremendous amount of advertising with all the local sports teams and even some for teams in other cities.

Whenever she requested tickets to a game, she was always provided with at least 4. The tickets would only be for the best seats, and sometimes, they would be for a suite along with all the catered food and drink you could enjoy.

Most of the time, Chris didn't care to go to the game, so that meant I could ask 3 of my buddies to the game. Since they were only the best of the best tickets and all my buddies knew this, none of them ever hesitated in accepting my offer!

Going to the games with my buddies was a real highlight for me, especially during the 10 years of surgeries, drugs, and all the setbacks, when I was at the lowest point of my life, seriously thinking that Chris and everyone would be better off without me.

Not that I would take my own life, knowing that would be the greatest sin to my faith, but maybe a natural death somehow, or even an accidental overdose, perhaps some sort of an accident, or even possibly natural causes considering my physical and mental health condition.

Thanks to the unconditional love, support, belief in me from all my loved ones, and the blessing of God, I made it through it.

# Chapter 14: The Escalation of Pain Medicine and More Surgeries

Within a few months after taking Vicodin numerous times daily, it became apparent the drug was having a minimal effect on reducing my pain.

The next narcotic prescribed was Percocet. Again, after a short time, the Percocet wasn't working for the pain. The following drug to be prescribed was Hydrocodone, and the same thing happened; after a while, I felt no relief.

Then I moved on to the drug that I would take for almost 10 years, Oxycontin. I was prescribed Oxycontin and a muscle relaxant named "Soma" to go along with it. They also prescribed Xanax. I think that was to help me from going crazy

**This narcotic combination would become my drug cocktail at the doctor's direction ... and the cause of my addiction that lasted nearly 10 years**.

The combination of Oxycontin and Soma is often referred to on the street as "Rich Man's Heroin." When taking Oxycontin and Soma together, their effect is the same as someone injecting Heroin; it's the same euphoria and mental state of mind.

After I was clean, I had a conversation with a pharmacist and we talked about the combination of drugs I was prescribed, including quantity and dosage, all in the name of pain management. As I spoke, I noticed he was really concentrating. Once I finished, he stated that in the pharmacy world, they called this combination of Oxy, Soma, and Xanax "The Holy Trinity ... be prepared to meet your maker".

It was strange that I took the exact same number of drugs every day, but the mental and physical intensity of the drug would affect me differently from day to day. Some days, I felt like I was functioning as a normal person… or that's what I thought. The people around me weren't thinking that. I've been told there were countless times when I was incoherent. Other days, I felt like a complete down-and-out drug addict.

**Once again, I should be dead, period!**

Let me provide some information on the drugs I was taking.

**Soma:** Carisoprodol also known by the name **Soma**, is a prescription skeletal muscle relaxant. It is typically prescribed to relieve some pain caused by muscle injuries like strains and sprains, stiffness, and spasms from surgeries. It blocks the pain sensations between the nerves and the brain. At higher doses, soma can lead to a euphoric high.

Soma is a schedule 4 controlled substance under the Controlled Substance Act. The drug comes in tablet form and is taken by mouth, often several times a day when treating an injury.

Combining Soma with opioids for even a minimally short time is a quick path to addiction and is life threatening.

On many occasions, when attempting to swallow my 4-tablet narcotic cocktail, one of the Soma would unexpectedly dissolve in my mouth before I swallowed it. When this happened, it would be the worst taste in my mouth possible, and it wouldn't go away for some time.

**Oxycontin:** Oxycontin is a strong prescription pain medicine that contains an opioid (narcotic) that's used to manage pain severe enough to require daily round-the-clock, long-term treatment.

Oxycontin is a schedule 2 controlled substance under the Controlled Substance Act. It's a narcotic analgesic that's widely used in clinical medicine (pain management).

This narcotic and all other narcotics comes an extremely high risk for addiction and dependency.

It can also cause respiratory distress and death when taken in high doses or when combined with other substances and alcohol.

My first surgery benefitted me for almost three years until another level of my spine (L4-L5) caused so much pain that it also required a spinal fusion. Just when I think I'm almost entirely recovered from one surgery, here we go again.

This time it was only a one-level fusion, and "Dr. Lance" performed the surgery at Sharp Memorial Hospital in San Diego in June of 2004. This procedure also required cutting through the muscle mass with another 8-inch incision and implanting new hardware, titanium rods, and bolts. Dr. Lance also removed the hardware from my prior surgery during this procedure. After three years, the bone cadaver that had been previously implanted at levels L2-L4 was fused entirely, and the hardware was no longer required.

A day or so after this surgery, Dr. Lance came into my hospital room to check on my condition. I was lying in bed watching the U.S. Open golf tournament, and Dr. Lance sat down on the side of my bed to watch the golf with me for an hour or so. During this time, we discussed my surgery, what to expect during recovery, and future rehabilitation plans.

From that point on, Dr. Lance and I had a special connection. I was confident I was in good hands and felt comfortable having him as my surgeon. Little did I know at the time that he would be cutting into me again three years later.

My rehabilitation period was expected to take up to 18 months. As it turned out, and with the experience of having already gone through major back surgery, I was able to get as good as I was going to get in about 8 months. I knew exactly how to push myself to the limit when it came to physical therapy. The recovery time was also shortened by going into aqua therapy straight after the surgery.

Unfortunately for me, in the Spring of 2007, my back was giving me more trouble. With my experience and knowing when something wasn't feeling right, I knew I was in trouble again.

I scheduled an appointment to go and see Dr. Lance once again to decide what type of treatment was needed to get me up and running again, so to speak.

We had a detailed Q&A during this appointment, and he conducted a few mobility tests on me. He said that the best way to tell what was going on with my back was to have an MRI performed.

I was hoping and praying that the MRI findings wouldn't require another surgery, but I knew in my heart that wouldn't be the case, and I was ultimately correct, making it my third major spinal surgery within 6 years.

After my first and second surgeries, where I was cut wide open, Chris had started researching to see if there were any new alternatives. She attended a few seminars at hospitals in the San Diego area, where she learned about new spinal surgical procedures. These were already being used in Europe and were beginning to be performed here in the U.S. These seminars were hosted by local neurosurgeons, describing the new "minimally invasive" surgery procedures and how these new techniques would significantly reduce the recovery time.

Before going to meet with Dr. Lance to discuss the findings of my recent MRI and what options were available for my treatment, Chris said, "If Dr. Lance isn't trained in this new minimally invasive surgery procedure, we'll seek another surgeon."

After the MRI was completed, we scheduled an appointment and went back to Dr. Lance to follow up on the findings. Right up until the appointment day, Chris and I agreed about our requirement for this new surgery technique.

When Dr. Lance came into the examination room and reviewed my MRI, he told us what needed to be done to correct my back. He explained that another level of my spine was damaged to the point of no return and needed to be fused—this time at the level of L5-S1.

Dr. Lance went on to explain that he had just recently returned from Europe, where he had been trained on a new surgical procedure currently being performed called "minimal invasive spinal surgery." Our prayers had been answered!

He explained that he only had to make two small incisions about three inches long each, one along each side of the spine with this type of surgery. There would be no cutting through the muscle mass, and they could still implant new and remove the old hardware, such as rods, screws, etc., required for a successful recovery. Minimally invasive surgery would also reduce my recovery period to approximately 6 months.

He felt I was a perfect candidate for this type of surgery, considering my age, my health, and the current condition at this level of my spine.

That's when Chris and I looked at each other, and we could see the pleasure and optimism in each other's eyes. Finally, a little bit of good news!

The doctor also informed us that he would be implanting flexible rods in my spine, significantly reducing the risk of other levels of my spine going out and needing medical attention.

The flexible rods allow the spine to bend at a particular level where they're implanted, reducing the amount of torque pressure on the spine while bending over. In my previous two surgeries, the rods hadn't been flexible. With the installation of flexible rods, it meant I would have a little more ability to bend over without putting extra stress and torque on my spine like the nonflexible rods did.

Dr. Lance and other neurosurgeons believed rods that don't flex contribute to the cause of different levels being damaged to the point of requiring surgery.

Here is an interesting fact describing the pressure ratio that's placed on your back when you lift items:

"It operates on a 10:1 ratio. Lifting an object weighing 10 pounds puts 100 pounds of pressure on your lower back. When you add the 105 pounds of the average human torso, you see that lifting a 10-pound object actually puts 1,150 pounds of pressure on the lower back."

So please always practice safe and proper lifting techniques. You don't want to go through what I've had to go through.

A large percentage of the residual pain that I have and will always have comes from scar tissue that has developed post-surgery due to the surgeon having cut through the main torso muscles and nerves. The build-up of scar tissue is significantly reduced with minimally invasive surgery.

Dr. Lance performed my third surgery in August of 2007. He removed the hardware from my previous surgery since that level was also completely fused, cleaned up what scar tissue he could, and installed the new flexible rods and the screws.

By this time, my physician at the pain management facility was prescribing me 240 Oxycontin, 240 Somas, and 90 Xanax a month. I guess the Xanax was just for shits and giggles!